SENSELESS

HOW POLITICS, RELIGION, AND LIBERALISM ARE DESTROYING AMERICA

DAVID CARROLL

INTRODUCTION

He, who allows himself to be insulted, deserves to be. - Pierre Corneille (1606 - 1684)

I have decided to start this book with my very own disclaimer clause. If you are one of the easily offended masses or a member of the politically correct elite, stop reading here, this book will not be a pleasant read for you and you will add it to your banned book list.

If you are still here and reading, I'm glad for many reasons, not least of which is that by you purchasing this book I make a little bit of money, a very little as it turns out. This book is basically my take on the state of the American landscape as seen through the eyes of a young middle-aged white male. I do not pretend to be insightful or deep, or even to have the answers to the topics that I discuss here, this is just a brief summary of how I see events surrounding me in my day-to-day life.

As many people do, I have had a dream to write a book. Seeing as that I read about two books a week, I thought that it would be if not easy, then not completely difficult, since I have experienced many different writing styles, so I should be able to combine them into a story format of my own choosing. Well after many starts, I had to stop, since I could only get to somewhere around page five and then I would run out of story to write. So these series of topics were chosen specifically since I can talk about the included topics to no end with a minimum amount of effort, although putting my thoughts to paper has proven to be almost as difficult as my prior book writing efforts have been.

These are not meant to be an all-inclusive list of what I see that I think is wrong or noteworthy, just those topics that I find common, and discussion worthy. Hopefully, this book will sell enough to warrant enough interest for me to be asked to write another one, in which I will try to include more in-depth analyst of specific issues and events.

Many thanks go out to all those that have helped me in this endeavor from simple encouragement, to the many discussions that I have had with many of them, and for the army of proofreaders. The opinions here are mine, as well as any errors or misunderstandings from my point of view.

From me to you, enjoy.

A BRIEF OVERVIEW

I have opinions of my own, strong opinions, but I don't always agree with them. - George Bush

Looking out across the nation, I see many that are content and comfortable to let the most vocal among if not the masses, then at least among the elite, to dictate policy for the country, with a total disregard for what is good for America, only caring about what is good for the person shouting that their policy is 'the best' or 'the only solution that makes sense', even if the underlying policy or position of the person voicing it, is opposite to or very bad for the person to whom the message is being sent or are voting to support those that voice any policy.

It is the rare person that votes for a candidate or policy stance, not of one's own party affiliation. The vast unthinking masses of the American electorate come to their party affiliation, not by any means of rational thought but more by what party one's parents belong to, or I think/support X and so does this political party, so I belong to this or that party, the opposite of this is also true in that I am opposed to whatever and that party supports that which I am opposed to so I MUST belong to the other party. These inherited party members or the one-issue members make up the lifeblood of both Democrat and Republican Party membership.

Politics is not black and white, or to be politically correct red and blue as the media and politicians themselves would have us believe, but shades of grey, or as the pc crowd would say purple. If for example, you support legal abortions, you must be against the death penalty and therefore a Democrat. What if I support both legal abortion and the death penalty, or I am opposed to both concepts, which party then should I support. For myself, I have a very complex system to chart the various candidates so I may cast my vote accordingly. I track my level of support and opposition to as many major and minor issues that come to my attention as possible. Next, to this, I track how the candidates that I have the opportunity to vote for in regards to their support and opposition to my list of issues and how they fall out. Finally, I cross-reference this to the political climate and movement of the political arena involved whether it is local, state or national in scope. So for an example, my pro-choice, pro-gun ownership, pro-death penalty, anti-national healthcare position may lead to different candidates at each level of elections and may be altered even more if a candidate is gathering too strong of support even as they endorse my core positions or are opposed to them. In other words just because candidate X supports this one position that I feel very strongly towards does not necessarily mean I will vote for him if his/her positions on other topics are in opposition to that which I believe. My support for the various topics and positions is tempered by my opposition to and willingness to accept less then total victory in one thing if it means accepting something else that I am or may be opposed to, just because a candidate supports my position on gun ownership will note guarantee my vote if that same candidate is opposed to my position on abortion or some other issue that I support. I as a concerned and informed voter strive for gridlock in Washington for I know that that is best for the country and that any change in the course of American policy must be done slowly and carefully over time to avoid major disruptions and catastrophe, much like piloting a large ocean-going vessel. Yes, this is very complex and yes, I do get this involved in the political debate, I take my right to vote both responsibly and very seriously. I know of way too many people that simply vote the party line every year and I shake my head in disgust and bewilderment thinking why do we even bother to have elections, politicians could care less about people like me and voters, while voters, on the whole, do not care about anything more than pulling a lever and thinking that they actually make a difference in the electoral process., because hey, it comes with a participation sticker, and in today's world, that's what is important. Politics has become nothing more than a series of useless and meaningless gestures used to manipulate the ignorant masses. Look at some of the recent political fora where candidates are throwing out glib phrases like 'The Straight Talk Express', 'Change', 'Hope', and others just as empty. What exactly, I want to know is 'Hope', and how is it going to make this country better, keep the economy growing, keep us safe, and all the other things that we look to government to do for us. I for one am all for hope, I hope every day, hope for meaningful lasting one night stands when I am alone and horny, hope for a better job or one that pays better, I am even hoping I can make a living writing. Hope is around all of us and is part of our daily lives; it is what gets most of us through when things are either at their bleakest or as a daily philosophy. Hope is many things to many people, what hope is not is a platform on which to base running a country upon. Another useless meaningless gesture being forced upon the American people in an effort to get someone elected is 'Change'. When I hear a politician talking about change, I start looking for my wallet, for I know that a) this so-called change is not going to benefit me and b) I am going to have to pay for it. Survey after survey shows, or claims, that Americans are fed up with our elected officials, yet how out-raged can we really be when we do or demand that absolutely nothing be done to fix or correct the abuses or excesses of our elected officials. The electorate has been reduced to the role of sheep in the political realm and those that have mastered the speech of emptiness are those that are elected.

In the latest campaign season, a season that lasts way too long by the way much has been mentioned about the age, sex, and race as the pillars and qualifications of the candidates to become president. As previously mentioned I am a little deeper in my selection for presidential candidate preference than the media inspired age/sex/race thing reminiscent of internet chat rooms. I look for more from my perspective leader of the free world. I like my candidate to preferably have views similar to mine, not that I want to impose any or all of my views upon others, but to be free to practice those of mine that do not violate the rights of others. Lacking that, a candidate that will not harm the country politically, economically, militarily and such is also acceptable. No wild changes of past practice and policy, to stand up for the rights of America and Americans, no negotiating with terrorists no matter the means they employ to pluck the heartstrings of the electorate.

Even the much-ballyhooed fourth estate (that would be the news media for those that do not know the word) have abandoned their role to inform us of the truth. This includes not only the mass media of newspapers and TV news but also includes the often-maligned new media of the Internet variety. Reporters and newscasters fail to ask serious propping questions of our elected and hope to be elected officials. Stories and past histories of a candidates views and voting record are omitted in the dialogue with the viewers, and each media voice is biased in the direction of the reporter/newscaster. Gone are the days of reporters actually digging for the truth and reporting it, a Nixonesque Watergate episode will never be reported in today's' media climate. Even when a politician is caught and the event makes the news, the story is instantly and easily forgotten by the media, never to be repeated when the offending politician runs again for election, they are not brought to task for any prior misdeeds. Truth in American politics is dead and has been for some time. To get the facts of a story or issue in an unbiased forum one must look to sources from outside the US. I remember many years ago a certain much loved American president was brought to task over some arms sale to some south/central American country and news feeding frenzy, sense of awe, and shock that was being reported in the American news media, I had known and been reading about it for over a year from a foreign newspaper and had more details and a much more in-depth analyst of the issue then any of US media outlet was reporting. I have to be honest here, it was not that I was specifically looking at foreign newspapers for information I was not getting from American news, I just happened to have a roommate from a foreign country and got the chance to read the paper from his home country that he had delivered to him, so he could keep up with the issues from home that were important to him. That was my first experience with finding and using non-American news sources to get the full story in if not an unbiased format at least one that was less biased in its slant Democratically or Republican in its reporting of a story.

One would think that with such easy access to alternative news sources, whether it be cable TV, foreign news shows and papers, and with internet access to other print and visual newscasting that news organizations would do more to reveal the truth and the facts of a story in an unbiased format, to dig for the truth, and ask politicians deep probing questions.

In America, we are served and served poorly at that, by the two main parties Republican and Democrat, with each party not only embracing but also expounding policy decisions based on the fringe/extreme elements of the party. Right wing conservative Christian Republicans want to destroy us by employing draconian religious doctrine as law and abandoning serious medical and scientific research, while left wing liberal democrats would destroy us by banning technology and embracing the extreme environmentalist agenda, no matter the cost and not only in dollars, but also in productivity and the un-quantifiably happiness index. I am all for a green, environmentally sound national policy, but I am unwilling to accept this at any and all cost. I can and do support the medical provision of doing no harm when it comes to environmental policy. I think we should leave the world better than we found it or at least no worse.

On global warming, I believe both that it is real and that it is part of a natural cycle with elements that we do not understand and cannot control. It is not the clean cut and dry issue that many 'Global Warming' protagonists would have us believe. To think that humans can control Global Warming and climate change is arrogant in the extreme. The environmentalist would have us believe that the release of CO2 in the atmosphere is the sole cause of all global warming and it is humans that are doing all of the releasing. Some minor facts on CO2 and CO2 emissions;

- CO2 makes up .05% of the entire atmosphere, to put that in perspective that would be 50 ¢ out of $1000
- Volcanoes outgas 15-20 times the amount of CO2 that humans produce every year.
- The exhaling of every living creature on the planet produces 10x more CO2 than all the human output.
- Dying and decaying vegetation (fall leaves, trees that die in the forest) produce more CO2 emissions that human burning of fossil fuels.

Unless these environmental activists that want to take our money for their pet projects have come up with a way to stop these other sources of CO2 emissions, I fail to see how me burning fewer gallons of gasoline per year is going to help the environment.

The environmentalist use of scare tactics is nothing new. They have been doing it for many years.

The planet was warmer and sea levels were higher during the Roman era. How do we know this you ask? Simple, by finding where the Romans came ashore when arriving in England, a place that by any measurement is many miles inland from the shoreline of today, England also boasted of vineyards in the area of London, a farm crop lacking today due to the inclement weather of today.

The environmentalists could claim that the Romans with all of their industry a releasing of CO2 into the air is what caused this pleasant climate that was experienced in the northern lands, but it would not be very believable unless we want to assume that the ancient Romans were as technologically advanced as ourselves. Some may believe a statement like that, but I would not put much faith in anyone who proposed an idea like that.

I also fail to see how they would plan to stop the natural events of an active earth and climate cycle. I think that for them to stop these natural events would be very detrimental to the planet.

There is also the minor issue of global warming that is being observed upon other planetary bodies in the solar system like Mars and Pluto (although technically no longer a planet. Are we humans the cause of these other observed cases of global warming? I for one fail to see any human activity upon these other planetary bodies.

It has been warmer in our past as seen in the Medieval Warm Period and during the Roman invasion of England, and it has been colder as during the period known as 'The Little Ice Age'.

The polar bears, the poster child of environmental global warming extremism, obviously survived this warmer period in our past, since they are still here today, meaning that the environmentalists claim that this will cause their extinction is a little far fetched and fanciful.

Intelligent energy policy is important, not because of global warming, but to balance the needs of developed and developing society. The environmental agenda of today is a ploy and scheme to redirect the wealth of the developed world to their own pockets while simultaneously keeping the developing world from reaching its full potential and enjoying the rewards of modern science and technology. Environmentalists are practicing a very modern form of slavery to protect the status of the elite at the expense of the very poor and middle class.

We are a technological society, and we do need to be smarter in how we use natural resources to ensure their future availability. This means employing manufacturing practices that use fewer resources, using those resources wisely, and minimizing waste and to include the recycling of products when we are done with them so that they may be made into newer products. We also need to realize and accept that the developing world will and do want what we have and take for granted. The worlds first world nations need to take these nations in hand and help them to build from scratch the infrastructure needed so that they can provide for their citizens that what we have and take for granted without them having to follow in our footsteps and making the same mistakes that we made. This will allow them to build green from the beginning without having to rebuild their societies to the new green standard of technology as we are now attempting to do. These developing countries need to be able to provide for their own people as much as we need to provide for ours. It is our role and responsibility to help them in this endeavor rather than continuing to exploit them as we are doing now and have done throughout our past. As we and other developed nations are being made painfully aware, it is far easier and cheaper to build green from the beginning than to have to rebuild as we are discovering. They have little or no infrastructure so for them, building green is easy and wise to set them upon this path now, providing that It will allow them to meet the needs of their people. We have spent billions on building, maintaining and upgrading our infrastructure, and now we are being told that we have to do it all over, not as it breaks done and comes to the end of its life but now.

The lines on this battlefield have been carved in stone so to speak, with liberals dominating the primary schools, and universities and with conservatives having their own religious school system and relying on over two hundred years of entrenchment into society and the institutions of society in just this country. It is within this realm that the battles themselves are being fought, with liberals trying desperately to separate American society from the grip of religious doctrine and the customs and traditions that have arisen during the course of our history.

A third entity has also been conceived to join into the fighting, and that is the charter schools that are becoming quite popular in large metro areas. Charter schools as near as I can tell are both an antithesis of the religious school and a more disciplined, controlled, and organized public school, where this will lead to in regards to educating our youth, or even to which side in the education war charter schools will align themselves with I am afraid to hazard guess at this point.

There are minor players in this the education war from parochial schools, boarding schools, military schools and the like, but the main battles are being waged in the more public educational arenas that we all know and are familiar with.

One such battle that I recently witnessed in the public school system was color day, all the students in a certain class or grade were required (requested) to wear a particular color shirt on certain days, i.e. red on Mondays, blue on Tuesday, green on Wednesday etc. whether this was meant to be a sly way to incorporate public school uniforms, much like private and religious schools or a sincere effort to unite the student body into a community of equality of sorts, I was and remain much opposed to this. Yes children can be cruel to each other and even perpetrate crimes against each other for or because of clothing, but suffocating the creativity, personality and personal expressions of those least able to stand up to and resist us the adults and leaders in society harms all of us and ill prepares these and all children for access to and acceptance of self into the world. Also noting that childhood criminal behavior in this or other areas is the fault of parents in the upbringing of their offspring, and punishing all children for the actions of a few and the failings of their parents send the wrong message to

On Politics

I have come to the conclusion that politics are too serious a matter to be left to the politicians. - Charles De Gaulle (1890 - 1970)

Politics is supposed to be the second oldest profession. I have come to realize that it bears a very close resemblance to the first. - Ronald Reagan (1911 - 2004)

Politics, from the Greek. poli meaning many and tics meaning, blood sucking leeches. Politics is the arena in which ideas come together to engage and to formulate the laws that govern a society. Politics in this country and in many others that have an educated populace has moved towards the left in ever-increasing steps. This is neither good nor bad just a fact of having an educated people. The opposite is just as true in societies that have an uneducated populace. Ignorance breeds ultra conservatism and codifying of religious doctrine into law, while education leads to new ideas and an advance away from religious doctrine as law. As an example of this, in my youth environmentalism was an extreme leftist liberal rallying, now everyone in the country no matter their political affiliation, rich or poor, business or private entity are becoming environmentally conscious, with recycling a fact of life in most towns and cities. Somewhere we as a nation have forgotten what politics purpose is, which is no more or less than to make the whole better while inflicting the least amount of chaos. Political and religious leaders today have demonized their opponents, and call them and those who follow them as unpatriotic. The great polarization of American politics is harmful to all American citizens and creates resentment that is not easily overcome. The two parties in American politics really need to split into their four respective parts, to make a better America for all, similar to the western European parliamentary democracies. In America, the liberalists are the leaders to drive America to an enlightened state. The Conservatives role is to maintain the traditions of society and our culture without as the saying goes 'throwing the baby out with the bathwater', it is left to democrats and republicans to define the battles lines and restrain the leftists and drag forward the conservatives. Democrats have abandoned their pledge to the poor by embracing policies that maintain the separation of race, sex, and social standing, such as diversification training, affirmative action, and by maintaining a welfare state through various entitlement programs. Their true ally is not the liberals that they have joined their future too but the conservatives, who support institutional infrastructure, both governmental and of the religious types that society maintains as its pillars. Republicans have the hardest job of all as politicians; they act as the brake on liberalist policy and must find the means to enact the good points of liberal thought with the economic interests of business and society, i.e. keeping the country productive and moving forward without bankrupting it though limitless entitlement spending. Ideas and ideals are the core concepts of politics, forcing your will upon the masses. Politics must have compromise otherwise it is just dictatorial rule, the majority may be what gets you elected but unless 100 % of the electorate agrees with you then you must factor the dissenters' opinions into any laws that you enact else when you find yourself in the minority your voice will not be heard. Also abuse can be easy if you fail to listen to the minority view, Opinionated talking heads from both sides scream at the top of their lungs no compromise on issue such and such, we the people must reject these fools and remind our elected officials (who by the way work for us) not to listen to these idiots. Compromise is not only good, but it is also what creates the rule of law and allows people from all backgrounds and walks of life to live together in a society and feel good about themselves. Compromise is also, what allows us to take that which is good or at least interesting, from those cultures, traditions, and societies that are different from us, and to accept and incorporate it into our society for the betterment of us all.

THE TWO-PARTY SYSTEM IN AMERICA

The more you read and observe about this Politics thing, you got to admit that each party is worse than the other is. The one that is out, always looks the best. - Will Rogers (1879 - 1935)[1]

Whilst doing research for this section I came across a number of websites listing and describing the various political parties here in the US and found some rather interesting sites. The first http://politics1.com/parties.htm listed many parties and their respective descriptions, some of which I found informative, humorous, and to be downright scary. For a much more inclusive list of parties and descriptions of each of them, I recommend http://en.wikipedia.org/wiki/List_of_political_parties_in_th

---

[1] Illiterate Digest (1924), "Breaking into the Writing Game"

e_United_States ,
http://dir.yahoo.com/Government/U_S__Government/Politics/Parties/ , or
http://www.votesmart.org/resource_political_resources.php?category=1 . A search on any of the popular search engines will also yield links to other sites and other information but these and the ones below offer a good starting point. I do not endorse any of these sites or any political party, but the Pan-Sexual Peace Party did get my attention though I must confess that I did not explore their website.

For those that seek to find more detailed information regarding the two main parties that one is likely to encounter and that garner the most attention in American politics I would direct you to either or both of the following websites; http://www.democrats.org/index.html and http://www.rnc.org/.

For the sake of brevity, let us start with the Democrats and their mission brief. This except for my commentary comes directly from their website.

The Democratic Vision[2]

The Democratic Party is committed to keeping our nation safe and expanding opportunity for every American. That commitment is reflected in an agenda that emphasizes the security of our nation, strong economic growth, and affordable health care for all Americans, retirement

---

[2] http://www.democrats.org/index.html - Democrat National Committee website

security, honest government, and civil rights. Also included is their plan, a bold new direction for a secure America. We seek:

Honest Leadership & Open Government – unless your last name happens to be Clinton or one of the almost 100% of current and past elected Democrats that got caught in the house banking and post office scandal during the early '90s

 Real Security – except if you actually live in this country, since the Democrats are willing to bow down and cower before any threat to America. Negotiation only works if you are dealing with honest people, and we know that honesty is a concept that is alien to Democrats.

Energy Independence – but without spending money on true works that will guarantee this, think nuclear or even tapping some of America's own reserves. I will even settle for allowing companies and even people to build wind turbines without some democrat crying that it might hurt the birds or it is an eyesore.

Economic Prosperity & Educational Excellence

Economic Prosperity – Higher taxes and wealth redistribution the policy the Democrats have been using so far does not create prosperity

Educational Excellence – unless it means actually educating our youth and teaching them to think or be able to perform even simple skills.

A Healthcare System that Works for Everyone – except for the doctors, nurses and pharmaceutical companies that provide this healthcare.

Retirement Security – Except that, we have no idea on how to pay for this except by using ever-larger percentages of the budget and increases in taxes. The government will provide for you no matter how useless you are.

The Republican Vision

Unfortunately, I could not find a similar statement on the Republican website, the closest thing that I found was the following.

Republican Principles[3] (My comments in italics)

I am a Republican Because...

I BELIEVE the strength of our nation lies with the individual and that each person's dignity, freedom, ability, and responsibility must be honored. – *I can agree with this.*

I BELIEVE in equal rights, equal justice, and equal opportunity for all, regardless of race, creed, sex, age, or disability. – *Except of course for those foreigners and*

---

[3] http://www.rnc.org/ - Republican National Committee website

non-Christians and any other people that we think are different from us.

I BELIEVE free enterprise and encouraging individual initiative have brought this nation opportunity, economic growth, and prosperity. – *And laws, integrity, and responsibility be damned.*

I BELIEVE government must practice fiscal responsibility and allow individuals to keep more of the money they earn. – *Only when we do not control the purse strings of the budget, we like to and can spend money just as good as any good Democrat can.*

I BELIEVE the proper role of government is to provide for the people only those critical functions that cannot be performed by individuals or private organizations, and that the best government is that which governs least. – *We really would prefer if you did not call on us for any reason, but needs must be met.*

I BELIEVE the most effective, responsible and responsive government is government closest to the people. – *We are not too good at it here either, but we believe it.*

I BELIEVE Americans must retain the principles that have made us strong while developing new and innovative ideas to meet the challenges of changing times. – *Except that we do not want to teach the children how to think for themselves and the (insert holy book of choice [The Bible preferred]) is the complete word of God, and we will tolerate no dissent on this topic.*

I BELIEVE Americans value and should preserve our national strength and pride while working to extend peace, freedom and human rights throughout the world. – *Even if it does means clubbing a few people over the head or shooting them to get our point across to them.*

FINALLY, I believe the Republican Party is the best vehicle for translating these ideals into positive and successful principles of government. – *If they truly believed like this and did this, without going all God starry-eyed and acted like responsible human beings without looking down their noses at the common man, I could support this.*

Way too much believe there for me to be comfortable with a political party, it sounds too close to that religious thing that they all seem to follow blindly.

The bottom line here is that they both sound wonderful until you realize that neither party explains in detail how they are going to do all the wonderful things that they say that they are going to do, or even what or how much it is going to cost. Even the much-maligned Ross Perot of a few years ago failed in this. His whole campaign consisted of pre-school colored charts and that he was going to have meetings to see what to do. Give me a plan, with real numbers and other facts and figures. I might not be able to understand the whole thing, but I will know that you have thought about it and have spent time on the issue and really do have a plan, not just something that sounds good. While I might not understand the whole thing there are people that might understand more of it or parts that I do not so we the people will know that you are not just blowing smoke at us.

As Lewis Black once said, 'the Democrats are a party of no ideas and the Republicans are a party of bad ideas'[4]. I don't know how much I agree with that statement as a whole, but I will agree that there are times that it comes closer to the truth than is comfortable.

Republicans have an image problem and it's not as Dennis Miller says 'nobody likes you'[5], it's much more fundamental than that. Here is a party that can trace its roots to opposing slavery and something like less than 10% of non-white America supports them. This is an image problem. It would appear to me that the Republican Party seems to have abandoned one of their aforementioned beliefs since they seem to have ignored non-white America while they climbed into bed with the religious right.

Democrats do not get off lightly here either. This party has recently, at least, adopted any leftist, socialist, environmentalist idea that someone gives breathe too, up to and including making up 'Global Warming' to scare us and steal our money for their wealth distribution program.

The two party system has failed us. The umbrella system of policy that each project leave out vast degrees and support for ideas that leave out room for debate and compromise. Unless one blindly follows either party, there

---

[4] Lewis Black – Black on Broadway (2004) DVD
[5] Unremembered album

is no room for rational thought among the issues. I would hazard a guess that aside form a few issues members in either party have no idea about the bigger picture and just follow the scare tactics that each side uses to scare voters away from the other side's platform.

Doing some more research I came across the following website uselections.com and found two interesting links in the FAQ section, asking am I a liberal and am I a conservative.

Am I a Liberal

Abolition of the death penalty

Believe in affirmative action

Belief in reinstating the Fairness Doctrine

Disapprove of teacher-lead prayer in classrooms & school-sponsored religious events

Equal opportunities for men and women in the military

Favor equal opportunity & denial of gender differences

Government-rationed & taxpayer-funded medical care (example: Universal Health Care Coverage)

The government spends big on social programs (also higher taxes to fund these programs)

Income redistribution (through progressive taxation)

Legalizing abortion & pro-choice

Legalizing same-sex marriages

Oppose an American foreign policy of continuous intervention

Oppose domestic wire-tapping & other intrusive acts (as authorized in the Patriot Act)

Oppose full private property rights

Support the protection of our environment

Support of labor unions

Support Globalism ("one world government")

Support obscenity and pornography as our First Amendment right

Support teaching comprehensive sexual education programs in schools (as opposed to abstinence-only programs)

Support a "Living Constitution" reinterpreted for modern times (not how it was originally written & intended)

Support disarmament treaties

Support gun control laws

Support government programs to rehabilitate criminals in society

The taxpayer-funded public education system

AM I A CONSERVATIVE

Actively support a return of prayer in schools

Believe in our Second Amendment 'Right to Keep and Bear Arms'

Believe that parents (not schools or teachers) should educate children about sex

Believe in a strong national defense

Economic allocative efficiency (as opposed to popular equity)

Endorse choice in education

Endorse lower taxes & tax cuts (favoring the upper class)

Favor the death penalty

Favor stronger law enforcement and anti-crime laws

Generally don't care much for the United Nations

Oppose same-sex marriages

Staunchly pro-life and want to stop abortions

Support free enterprise

Support limited government

Support strong public morality

Support laws against pornography & obscenities

Support enforcement of current immigration laws

Support private medical care & retirement plans

Support the tightening of our border security

Want to open foreign markets to products made in the USA

Want to weaken or eliminate failed social support programs

Even I, as well read, and as knowledgeable that I am had a few problems with some of the phrases (questions) posed In these definitions and had to look them up. I made my own list and question just who represents me and people like me or even the people that are opposite of me or any of the wide variations of people that neither of these two ideologies that exist out there fit into.

SO IN FAIRNESS, MY IDEOLOGY LIST

Disapprove of teacher-lead prayer in classrooms & school-sponsored religious events

Equal opportunities for men and women in the military

Favor equal opportunity, but not a denial of gender differences (as men and women are different and have different strengths and weaknesses that we need to be aware of and take into consideration)

Legalizing abortion & pro-choice

Legalizing same-sex marriages

Support the protection of our environment (meaning using responsible methods for mining, drilling, lumbering, fishing, waste disposal). I like national parks like

Yellowstone, or being able to swim in the ocean, fish and drink river water. My own environmentalism is to be a good neighbor, do as little harm as possible and put things back.

Support Globalism ("one world government") – I'm biased here and think that the US system is the best and that this world government should be based upon our system and laws, but I truly believe that for man to reach the stars and explore the galaxy in any meaningful way we need to stop finding better ways to kill each other and work towards treating all humans on earth equal ensuring life, liberty, and pursuit of happiness. This is not to say that other countries don't have good things also, just that I am most familiar with the US way of things, I'm more than willing to accept and even adopt things that are better than what we have here.

Support obscenity and pornography as our First Amendment right

Support teaching comprehensive sexual education programs in schools (as opposed to abstinence-only programs), and yes abstinence should be a part of it because many do first engage in sexual activity before they are ready emotionally, physically, mentally, primarily because we reach puberty before we reach maturity. I also believe that parents should also play a part in educating our children in regards to sex as parents know their children best and can answer questions that they might not feel comfortable asking a stranger (teacher) or in front of their peers

The taxpayer-funded public education system, conversely I'm opposed to special interests (namely religious groups demanding non-science taught in our science classes, and the rewriting of history to be more politically correct).

Believe in our Second Amendment 'Right to Keep and Bear Arms'

Believe in a strong national defense

Endorse lower taxes & tax cuts (favoring the upper class), coupled with reduced spending. All tax cuts should be equal in terms of percentage not in actual amount, 1% is equal in percentage even if it's not equal in actual amount.

Favor the death penalty

Support free enterprise

Support limited government

Support enforcement of current immigration laws – I'm actually for stronger laws and tougher enforcement

Support private medical care & retirement plans – not that there is not a role for government to supply and or supplement those in the private sector

Support the tightening of our border security

Want to open foreign markets to products made in the USA

Want to weaken or eliminate failed social support programs

I hope and wait for the day when someone creates a schism within either or both of the US's main political parties to more truly reflect the views of the people. In all honesty, I see this happening to the Republican party sooner rather than later before it happens to the Democrat party. Whichever side it happens to first though will be a boon to the country as a whole and lead to great changes in how we progress forward. This is not to say that the new party will gain prominence overnight, but I do believe that it will enact a shift in the political balance and alter the governmental landscape.

I propose a new Republican party that supports fiscally sound policies, one that is socially accepting of homosexuals among others, that doesn't use religious doctrine to dictate its policy, that is accepting of sound science, that listens to and fights for the people and not corporate or special interest groups. One whose policies encourage people to take responsibility for their actions to limit government intrusion in our lives, to not treat Americans as criminals, to secure our borders, to provide for a strong national defense, that treats all Americans as equals, limits both the number of immigrants and types of immigrants that we allow in, and even goes so far as to expel those here illegally. Fines for persons and businesses that hire illegals should be far stiffer than they currently are, including jail time, large fines and loss of business license for those businesses caught employing illegals.

ON RELIGIONS AND SCIENCE

A MYTH IS A RELIGION IN WHICH NO ONE ANY LONGER BELIEVES. - JAMES FEIBLEMAN

THE MORE I STUDY RELIGIONS THE MORE I AM CONVINCED THAT MAN NEVER WORSHIPPED ANYTHING BUT HIMSELF. - SIR RICHARD FRANCIS BURTON (1821 - 1890)

SCIENCE IS ORGANIZED KNOWLEDGE. - HERBERT SPENCER (1820 - 1903)

Science is the driving force for any technological society, not just an advanced civilization like ours. Science is what allowed ancient civilizations to build the pyramids of Egypt, the Colossus of Rhodes, even the laying of roads in the Roman Empire to name just a few of the buildings and structures that a knowledge of science can give a society. These buildings and structures even modern ones such as space telescopes, mapping the genome of the species and CD players are the result of science. It is scientific knowledge, not religious knowledge or belief in a deity that has achieved all of this.

In our modern world, the more that science finds answers for, the more that people come to the realization that the educational system has failed. These people and others of the under-educated masses feeling alone and lost in the world are turning to the various religious and philosophical teachings available in an effort to bring meaning, understanding, and validation in their lives. Many of these the under-educated among us are the first to ask such questions as 'Why do we fund space research (or some other such scientific endeavor)' without knowing about the benefits and advances that such research and exploration has imparted unto their lives. Space research has led from the complex such as M-theory, a better understanding of cosmic events, or even the composition of matter itself, to the mundane, such as better building materials, improved telecommunications, health, and medical discoveries, CDs, portable music players and cell phones barely larger than a deck of playing cards. With each realm of scientific study that we pursue, the findings from these various studies, help to improve the lives of everyone, from new materials, medical breakthroughs, new technology, better understanding, and knowledge of our world, be it from geological for building better buildings, to emergency preparedness from early storm warnings.

The grim determination that many people exhibit to hold tight to bronze-age mythology or new-age mysticism, is more than a knee jerk reaction away from the world in which we as a technological society live and exist, but as a complete rejection to hundreds of years of scientific study and thousands of years of technological advancement. This is most frightening, to say the least, and the creative ways and means that the religious among us create and expound this rejection of science and technological advancement is frightening. These methods include not only the completely absurd but also their almost limitless various pseudo-scientific theories and explanations to help them to justify their irrational belief. This behavior on their part ranks among if not, the most useless wasting of human knowledge and endeavors ever to be conceived. When mankind was ignorant of the most basic and simplest of scientific concepts such as fire or why is the sky blue and why does it rain etc, a belief in deities and the supernatural, was if not justifiable, is at least understandable though still an unforgivable explanation of how and why the world around us is and functions.

Most, if not virtually all theists, accept the validity of science, if not the conclusions of science. They are even apologetic of science saying such inane things as maybe or that is how (insert the name of your deity of choice here) did something or the other. It is usually when science breaks the bounds of the mundane or is completely opposite of or at odds with religious texts and understanding that theists become the loudest and most outspoken against science and the supposedly morally empty world that science offers. One example of this that comes to mind happened many years ago during a conversation about the Library at Alexandria.[6] The conversation went something like this, one person commenting on the wonder of the library and the contents

------

[6]

of its collected works was in awe of such a great project, his companion stated the building was only an indication of man's folly, since either the works encased within supported the sacred religious text, and therefore were thus irrelevant and redundant or they were in opposition to the the sacred religious text, in which case they were blasphemous and should be destroyed (an event that should be noted actually occurred to the Library at a later date.

This minor example shows the limited scope of education and educational tolerance that is often displayed by most religious followers and their organizations. The library could contain books on boat building, the actual building of one, not just instructions of go build one this big like is stated in the Bible, a text that would neither support the bible or be in opposition to it. Religion has shown this intolerance to science and education time and time again and been shown to be wrong more often than it has been right.[7] [8]

Religion and religious belief, no matter the sect, have adapted a core precept, embracing a certain fundamental level of ignorance and obedience to that ignorance as twin pillars to and of religious belief itself. That precept being, to believe without evidence or proof of the super-natural that is called god. Religion starts with the premise that god exists and goes from there that everything from

---

[7] Galileo was placed under house arrest for disagreeing with the church statement that earth was the center of the universe and that all other heavenly bodies were perfect spheres.

[8] It was a priest, who was also an amateur astronomer that convinced Einstein to re-look at his statement of a static universe.

atoms to zebras and everything in between proves the existence of a god and the truth and accuracy of the chosen religious text of the adherent. We demand proof of any other claims of the extraordinary from bigfoot and the Loch Ness monster or even ghosts, before believing in them, so why is it that with religion that we accept belief before and even without proof, or even when proof contradicts the religious claim?

Science and the scientific method at least have the means for others and outsiders to test the conclusions and results of the experiments, in a word it is falsifiable. Science at the upper reaches of cosmology may be approaching philosophy with the latest theories such as p-theory, m-theory and the existence of branes and their resultant collision that created the universe that we live in. These theories are not testable or falsifiable since we cannot (as of yet at least) recreate and or observe the creation of this or any other universe. These theories have the math behind them to back up the assertions being made by them, and anybody willing to learn the necessary mathematics can test the accuracy of the assumptions being made though I doubt the technology will ever be made to run an actual experiment, though the existence of other universes may be testable at some time.

I for one cannot say for certain that this or that or any god or gods exist or do not and have never and never will exist, but I feel that it is much better to question and test and probe the reaches of the universe for all the hows and whys possible than to simply say 'God did it' for even if it turns out to be true that some deity or other supernatural being did, in fact, do it, a revelation that will only be learned after our deaths and will have no bearing to us beforehand, the how and why are just as, if not more important than the act itself. I must also state here that upon careful examination of the universe from the cosmological scale (i.e. the very big) to the subatomic scale and all places within using many different means (visual, microwave, radio wave telescopes) and from the examination of creatures here on earth from their DNA structure up to the whole creature including dissection, I have found no evidence of any of the millions of gods that man has worshiped in his history.

ON RELIGION

One can question when or whether Judaism itself will fall from the level of true religion to that of sect or even to cult status, as the number of adherents of that faith as a percentage of religious followers as a whole continues to shrink. Or is this a case were Judaism as the mother branch of western monotheism will protect its status as a true religion? Given it's status as the state religion of one country that may be enough to protect its status for the time being, but it may come into question if/when Judaism falls from being the dominant religion of Israel, a possibility since various Christian sects and Islam are practiced there.

People look on religion as a good and wonderful thing and point to the work with the poor and impoverished as signs of the goodness of religion. People fail to look at or acknowledge all of the bad that accompanies religion, the terrorists, the pogroms and prosecutions, the shackling of scientific thought and of the scientists themselves. It is one thing to want to lead a life that is good and holy by one's own religion and by the definition of what that entails, it is quite another to force that desire upon others who may or may not believe as you do, or even want to live up to the same standard that you have set for yourself.

I must comment on Mother Teresa here. She was much more a friend of poverty than to the poor being quoted as saying that it was good that the poor suffered as it helped the world. When she did become ill, it was off to the best medicine and doctors the world could provide and money to pay for, while the poor that she administered suffered from poor food, in cramped unclean spaces, often with no relief from the pain as modern painkillers were not provided.

To want to or to dictate though official state policy that is so is not only criminal but is an affront to humanity and insulting to the deity that is claimed to have made all of life in the first place. In all religions it is the worshipped deity that makes the decision of whom is allowed into the eternal bliss of heaven or whatever the good and holy are rewarded with is called, the god(s) do not need or want the help of the creation to assist in what they will deem is worthy, and are quite willing to let the unworthy be punished or abandoned in the afterworld (life).

Even as a small child I lacked belief in any creator greater than my own parents, it should also be noted that I lacked a belief in Santa Clause, the tooth fairy, Easter Bunny, and all other make believe fantasy creatures that accompany youth and childhood. This lack of belief did not in the least make my childhood any less enjoyable in any way possible, and it was not for a lack of trying on my parents' part, they even had to tell me not to break the news (truth) to my younger siblings and my older ones that still believed in these mythical entities. No one told me that these were not real; they were just things that I never believed in, presents under a tree or money under the pillow was not proof of the existence of the associated entities and a belief in any deity never managed to take hold no matter how often I was dragged to church.

Seeing and listening to little children saying things of a religious nature such as the ever-popular Christian mantra 'Jesus loves me, this I know', makes me cringe. I have trouble accepting that society not only allows this to happen but also accepts it and thinks that it is cute to see helpless little children abused in such a way. Parents that do this to their children should see the inside of a jail cell for inflicting these types of abuses upon so small a mind. To seek solstice in religion as an adult with the ability to think and have rational thought and make a conscious choice to do so is one thing but to forcibly brainwash, a child is quite another.

At one time, it might even have been justifiable to indoctrinate our children into our religion to give them a sense of community and belonging. Those days sadly or joyfully are long gone though. In our modern world with people moving to different cities, states, and even countries altogether, for work, for school, or for love, the continued forced, one could almost say mandated religious indoctrination of our youth can not only interfere with their ability to succeed in this world that we have created for ourselves but is in itself morally and criminally and ethically wrong.

How and why humans maintain the same basic deity belief system that originated almost 6000 years ago with only two major modifications amazes me. The Jewish faith which spawned both of the modifications

(Christianity and Islam) originated in a world very different from our own in both knowledge and science, yet these three schools of thought have progressed through time to the modern area almost completely unchanged from their original works. Medical knowledge has gone from an era where fairly minor injuries could be merely crippling to mortal even with the best treatment to were we are today of being on the brink of being able to regenerate whole limbs. Today's medical profession can save people from horrific injuries that by all rights the person should be dead from yet in a matter of months they are often back on their feet and living as if the injury never occurred. We have drugs today that can prevent and cure diseases that would have been fatal even a few short decades ago. We have telescopes that can look to the farthest reaches of the universe and see how the universe looked millions of years ago. Engineers can build machines on the molecular level and construct buildings that rival mountains in size. We can manipulate light to communicate sound and store vast amounts of information. We have built craft and sent them hurtling out into the vastness of space and they have traveled farther than anything else man has ever sent in motion. We have stepped upon another world and are poised to step upon yet another. Other scientists can read the blueprint of life and map the genome of the species. Grade school students today perform feats that the greatest of scientists and thinkers would not have believed possible a mere century ago.

Yet through all these wonders and advancements that man has achieved, a majority of the human race is still clinging desperately to a believe system of god(s), angels, and demons and these belief structures have gone through almost no change since they were first conceived of and have provided nothing to help, benefit, or advance humankind.

Religion told us not to bath, to keep away the demons and for all our efforts, we received the plague to ravage life and kill almost a third of the population. Meanwhile, science told us to bath regularly to wash away germs and we are rewarded with longer life, the better chance of survival from our wounds. Religion placed the earth, and a flat one at that, at the center of the universe, then the galaxy, and finally the solar system, and yet again science proved that this too was incorrect with the earth being just one more planet circling just one more sun in the vastness of space and was not special in any way other than it being our home. For all the fallacies and falsehoods that religion has made us believe when all of it goes against all common sense, and yet religion is not an easy beast to slay.

With the number of times that religion has been shown to be wrong in its stance and position on so many issues, it is no wonder that the highest educated among us through out the world have adopted atheism or its cousin agnosticism for the default in regards to the god position. For education will set you free while ignorance will keep you enslaved. It is no surprise then that industrialized countries have the highest percentage of non-believers, while non-industrialized countries have an almost universal god believe and have tied the state into the religious belief system.

I make no distinction between the various religious beliefs and its associated deity. To me, Zeus, Thor, God, Jesus, Allah, and YHWH, to name just a few are all the same and hold no special interest, place of importance, believability, or power for me. The stories attached to these figures are at best fantasies and fables the same as the famous Aesop but much more dangerous due to the ingrained belief in the supernatural that they entail. If one must turn to philosophy or teaching to bring meaning to one's life, I for one would prefer them to adopt one of the Eastern philosophies like Buddhism. The incredulity of the western style invisible father figure in the sky type is insulting and degrading to mankind in general and intelligence in particular. Western religions, all are based ultimately on the basis that daddy will punish you if you misbehave (and by misbehaving, we mean fail to follow the teachings exactly). Followers of western religions for whatever first brought them to their particular faith continue in this belief fallacy from fear, fear of missing out on some un-supported promise of a reward, fear of punishment from an un-provable, un-needed creator deity, and lastly fear of abandonment from other than continue to follow the faith.

Religious followers are so focused on an after-life, that none of them can even prove exists, and it's rewards and punishments that they fail to work to improve this world and enjoy the one life that we all know and can prove exists. Denying oneself of pleasure does not make one enjoy one's existence more and in my experience actually makes life more stressful and aggravating than if one had just partaken of the pleasure in the first place. There are exceptions to this of course but as a general rule, it holds true.

My, for lack of a better word, morals stem not from religion, rather from my own sense of self-worth and community altruism. These morals have kept me from a number of jobs and have brought me into conflict with those around me, but I can look myself in the eye or in the mirror and feel proud of who I am and not ashamed of any deed that I have done or how I may have treated someone.

I, unlike Jews and Catholics, do not have guilt for my actions or inactions. I am not accusatory judgmental like Christians and Muslims. Also unlike religious followers of most faiths, I do not feel compelled to forcible convert one to my point of view, I am content to engage one in dialogue and let one come to my stance though time and education when they are ready too. I would rather have someone support my position because they not only feel as I do but understand what they are supporting and have been given the information needed fully and truthfully rather o having them adopting my position out of fear, ignorance or deceit.

It is too easy to deceive a person that lacks your knowledge of a subject, or if you are coming from a position of power or influence over another. Children are especially easy to deceive and are vulnerable to deception for they lack the experience in dealing with people that adults have acquired simply by life experience. They also expect truthfulness and honesty from those that are teaching them since we have learned to expect those traits from those that are teaching us and/or have a position of influence over us such as parents do, to have our best interest in mind and treat us as such. Parents teach us that minor injuries, like cuts and scrapes, are just that, minor and okay and nothing to panic about, that's why mom's kisses on a boo-boo make the hurt go away. They teach us not to fear going down the slide and other such lessons so we are in a sense programmed from an early age to trust and look to them for guidance. It is not until religious instruction that even the best parents fail miserably in the care and rearing of their children. They indoctrinate them into their faith out of fear, habit, and social pressure to conform to society's religious bias.

It is amazing to me the amount of insecurity that is felt among the religious community in regards to their confidence and comfort within their religion. I have often questioned the strength and depth of their commitment to religion when they feel the need to surround themselves and place reminders of their god upon just about every surface. They have tagged the currency of this country with a reminder of their god, they place religious symbols and icons in public buildings and squares, Engrave phrases and biblical passages upon those buildings and other such activities that amount cloaking themselves in religion to remind themselves of their religious belief.

Take for instance in this country the phrase 'In God We Trust' that is emblazoned upon our currency. Was this phrase placed upon American currency from the founding of the country? No, it was added later at the request of the religious establishment starting in the mid-1860s during a time when we were fighting a civil war and with both sides claiming that god was on their side, and did not become universal on all currency until the early 1900s. Even the pledge of allegiance, written by a Baptist minister[9] lacked the words under god for over 50 years. The original pledge, written in August of 1892 was *'I pledge allegiance to my Flag and the Republic for which it stands, one nation, indivisible, with liberty and justice for all.'* The word "to" was inserted later that year in October to have it then read 'I pledge allegiance to my Flag and **to** the Republic for which it stands, one nation, indivisible, with liberty and justice for all.' This was but a minor change that did not alter the meaning of the pledge. The next change to occur and a major one at that, took place in 1923 and 1924 during the National Flag Conference, under the 'leadership of the American Legion and the Daughters of the American Revolution, they changed the Pledge's words of 'my Flag,' to 'the Flag of the United States of America.' Bellamy disliked this change, but his protest was ignored. Now after 30+ years the pledge read as *'I pledge allegiance to the Flag of the United States of America and to the Republic for which it stands, one*

---

[9] Francis Bellamy - http://history.vineyard.net/pledge.htm

nation, indivisible, with liberty and justice for all.' This was done during a period of high immigration and insured that immigrates were pledging allegiance to the correct flag, a definite plus in these changing times. The latest change was to occur in 1954, after a campaign by the Knights of Columbus, Congress added the words, 'under God,' to the Pledge. This latest change makes the Pledge as now written both a patriotic oath and a public prayer. This is a clear violation of the Amendment baring the establishment of or recognition of religion by the state. It in effect makes mandatory the belief in a deity, specifically one called god (only Christians so far refer to their deity simply as god) to be a true citizen of this country and to hold office or testify in trial as the 'So help me God' utterance is a common if not universal phrase at all of these occurrences. Although the swearing of an oath of honesty to a deity like the phrase 'So help me God' is not mandatory for the most part, it is the default position and is the government's tactic admission of the supremacy of a deity over this country and our lives. This can be argued as a violation of the separation clause that is in the constitution. Whether the Supreme Court would hear a case is another matter, all together and it should be noted that they have concluded in the past that 'In God, We Trust' does not indeed violate the constitution. I think that they are in error on this but I have no say or control in this and like opinions and certain body parts, everyone has one and often they often offensive to others.

As has been shown many times in the course of American history, this country was not founded upon Christian beliefs as many in the religious community insist, but rather in the belief that man can govern himself wisely all on his own. At best, it can be claimed that many of the founding fathers were deists as well as more than a smattering number of atheists. Whether the deists among them were Christians, Jews or some other religious sect, we may never know. What we can infer from their work is that it was not their intent for this to be a Christian country or one run by the tenets of any specific religion. We know this, for the simple reason that they specifically barred the state from recognizing any religion in our constitution and omitting any references to religious law within the judicial system that they left us with.

Our founding fathers would be very disappointed in us, in what we have allowed our government to become. This is not just in how much we have allowed religion to color our legal system and influence our scientific establishment, but also how much we have allowed the government to intrude into our lives. Ben Franklin once said 'He who would give up liberty for freedom deserves neither', though to be honest this is a mis-qoute and was in reference to a very specific event, while Thomas Jefferson said 'A government large enough to give it's people everything is also large enough to take anything away'. We accept these intrusions with nary a thought of their consequences. We mandate the use of seatbelts in cars for safety not because they assist us to be better drivers. We penalize smokers while maintaining the legality of tobacco (maybe the government learned from its folly with the enacting of prohibition). Government is also mandating this fat or that fat type in our food over others, purely in the interest of health, never mind what the consumer wants and is willing to pay for. There are even communities seeking to ban restaurants for the simple fact that they serve fattening foods or banning non pc fare (like foie de gras). To insure the safety of our children riding bikes, helmets must now be worn by all riders (I think it is all since I never see a helmetless rider anymore). When I was a child, the only kids that wore helmets while riding a bike were those that were in special education and could not be trusted to not run their bikes into walls and other objects anyway. We have also turned over our retirement to the government with the government providing 1/3 to ½ of the income of most retirees in the form of social security; this does not include Medicaid and other benefits to the elderly. We even give the elderly school and property tax breaks. I once saw a political cartoon that depicted the middle class carrying the poor on their backs with the rich sitting on the shoulders of the poor; I think that it needs to be updated to place the elderly on the shoulders of the poor with the rich on their shoulders. More and more burdens are placed upon the middle class of this country and Democrats now want them to foot the bill for insuring everyone in the country. This would be in addition to all those that they currently cover, their own families, the elderly through Medicaid, the poor through Medicare, the elderly and poor through other government programs, in my state it is called child health plus. I ask who else is left, or is it that by providing insurance coverage to just about everybody else in the country that we have neglected to provide any for ourselves or cannot afford insurance for ourselves. I already work something like five months of the year just to pay my existing tax burden between all the different taxes (Federal all forms [Income, SS], State, School, Local), not to mention gas taxes, phone taxes and phone usage taxes to provide schools (?) with internet access (why schools don't pay for this themselves out of their own budgets, I hazard to guess), usage fees for hunting, registering a car the list is almost endless. The government has even more ways to take your money than you do in the earning of it.

I do not mind helping a person out when they are down on their luck. It is the entitlement mentality, which I am opposed to. I am sick of hearing things like; I am black, I am a woman, I am a single parent, I am old, or any of the hundreds of other excuses used to demand a government handout. I work my ass off to provide for my family, and it is annoying to see those on the dole living better than those that work at the lower rungs of the economic scale. Why should a person collecting a government handout live better than a person working a 40hr/wk job, even if it is a minimum wage job?

The total value of all governmental handouts to the non-working poor should not exceed that of a person working minimum wage at a 40 hr/wk job. Realistically it should not exceed 75-80% of that amount.

On Marriage

Much has been said in the media and around the water cooler about what is or what is not marriage. It has even been proposed to incorporate what marriage is into the constitution. Before that can be considered, we must ask and answer the question of what is marriage. So let us start this discussion. Historically speaking we have examples of a man and women joined together as marriage, there are many instances of a man with multiple wives and that too is marriage, there are even cases of a woman with multiple men that is called marriage. There may even be cases of multiple men and women in a single union that is marriage. Why then are we limiting the definition of marriage to include just one man and one woman? Marriage at its basis is simply the union of people for social and economic benefit. Marriage has existed since before religion, on that basis alone why then limit the definition of marriage to only that which is approved by religion? When two people, a man and a woman in these examples, decide to join together in an attempt to live out their lives together and hopefully produce children, we call that marriage. In the upper echelons of society, we have unions of convenience, a woman will seek a man of power, wealth or political savvy, to provide for her and her/their offspring, this too is called marriage even if love does not enter into it. The reverse is also true here for men, with a man seeking a wife to secure his place on the rungs of power. In aristocratic families, and we have our own form of aristocracy here in the US, unions occur to secure wealth and produce an heir to carry on the family name or to inherit the family fortune, this is also called marriage. Some unions produce no children, because of fertility reasons of the couple, advanced age, or they may have children from prior unions and desire no more, or the couple may not desire children at all, or even health reasons of either partner, yet we still call these unions marriages. Here in these examples, it is not the situation or cause of the union that makes a union be labeled as a marriage, we apply it to all of these joinings, emotional attachment and/or offspring are not the cause for the labeling. Maybe it is the place of the union or the overseer that brings the label to marriage. Who can perform a marriage? A short list is clergy members (priests, rabbis, imams), judges (justice of the peace), ships captains at sea in certain water conditions, state-sanctioned marriage officiators (of a non-religious type). Now here we have marriage as both a religious and a secular institution, and we call the resulting couples from either union as married. To further complicate matters a Catholic or any religious follower could marry someone of a different religion or someone of no religion and the resulting union is still called a marriage by society and is recognized as a marriage within society. There are religious institutions that don't officially recognize such unions as marriage but they still treat the members of these unions as married couples and accord them the same rights, responsibilities, and courtesies as if both partners did share the same religion. These religious institutions also recognize the unions performed by other religious or secular institutions granting members of those unions the same courtesies as if they were members of that religious institution. All of these unions are granted the same legal rights, responsibilities, and courtesies and are all called marriage by all parties involved. We even have states where a couple that lives together for a number of years as a joined couple have what is known as a common law marriage, there is no paper to signify this union, no ceremony, nothing to make known to the outside world that these people are in fact married, yet they are granted the same rights and responsibilities as those couples that do go through the more public means of union whether it is by a clergy or member of the judiciary. The rights of survivorship, inheritance, child custody and other next of kin rights are granted to all of these couples without question, and few if any obstacles. A policy of separate but equal in referring to gay marriage as a civil union opens the door to in-equality to the couples. It allows for the placement of restrictions on what a gay couple can do and receive in the eyes of the law. Would a civil union as applied to gay couples place restrictions on adoptions that are not placed upon heterosexual couples or even on singles that seek to adopt a child or children. How would the issue of custody come into play in either divorce or death of a parent in a gay civil union? By making separate definitions and terms for heterosexual unions and for gay unions open the door to discrimination. Marriage either secular or religious automatically grants certain rights and responsibilities to the couples involved. Opening the definition of marriage to include gays in describing two people who voluntarily join together for social and economic stability will be the natural evolution of the word once gay couples are accorded the same right to marriage and happiness as non-gay couples whatever a court decides is the definition of marriage. Time alone will alter the definition of the word marriage.

Now there are some that want to make it not only acceptable but also legal to discriminate against people in matters of the heart when it is forbidden by law and custom to do so in other arrangements. If I am, renting or selling a property I cannot discriminate based on a persons skin color, size of family, national origin, sexual orientation, age, religion, or sex. The same goes for employment practices, granting of loans from a bank, accepting students into a university or the military. In every aspect of life that I can think of, I am forbidden from discriminating against someone due to his or her age, race, religion, sex, sexual orientation, or nationality, or disability. I can't even run an all-male school if I accept government money as was shown in the very public Virginia Military Institute case that was brought a number of years ago, yet somehow churches are not bound by the same restrictions in discrimination when they are accepting government monies. I even question the legitimacy of the United Negro College Fund and their policies, do they get any government funds and do they give scholarships to non-Negros, how and why is it that they are allowed to discriminate? What would the ACLU say to the United Caucasian College fund or even the United Oriental College Fund.

Discrimination is outlawed in so much of our society yet a select group wants to mandate discrimination against others purely on that person's sexual orientation, that is wrong, maybe we as a secular nation should make it illegal for a person with a theistic belief from holding public office; only atheists can be elected to positions within government as the opposite is the case in at least one state.

I have even heard some proposals to restrict marriage of gays and lesbians to those couples that have been together for a set amount of time, or that have met some other arbitrary hurdle, yet heterosexual couples have no obstacles in their way, in some states two people can meet while having breakfast and be married by lunch, why then should homosexual couples be more restricted or more committed to each other than heterosexual couples in regards to marriage. I am not advocating people of whatever sexual orientation to rush into marriage but I oppose restricting one over the other.

It may be time for a few new sects one for each of Christianity, Judaism, and Islam, the sect of the homosexuals, since religious institutions by default recognize the unions of the other sects and religions. All it would seem to require is a male in his 30's to found a new church. I only mention that since history has shown us that most western religions seem to be founded on the teachings of a male in his 30's, Abraham of the Jews was a young man of middle age, Jesus was 30 when he started his teachings, Mohammad was under 40 when he started his teachings, most of the founders of the Reformation that split the Catholic church were males in their 30's, even Brigham Young of the Mormons was under 40. Religion it would appear is a middle-aged man's game.

Some argue that it's not the role of government to change the definition of marriage to include homosexual unions, and I agree, it is also not the role of government to define the definition of a word, usage defines a word's definition, just as the word cool has many definitions, because of its usage, marriage too can have a broader definition to include homosexual unions as well as the various heterosexual ones. No one is arguing that a religious institution has to perform a marriage between homosexuals, just as no one is arguing that certain religious institutions have to accept female priests, preachers, rabbis, imams, etc. Religious institutions are allowed to dictate their own policies for who can belong and those that run counter to the wider social norms and acceptances can, will, and do see their memberships decline and even the schisms that develop within them as has happened from the protestant Reformation within the Roman Catholic church to more recently the divisions happening with the Anglican church.

"Separation of church and state" has become a fighting phrase, largely because of disagreement about how far to carry the concept. But nearly all Americans agree on the institutional separation of church and state. Yet with respect marriage, we do not maintain even institutional separation. Marriage combines religious and legal institutions; it is our most fundamental breach of separation of church and state.

Marriage is both a religious institution and a legal institution. It is jointly administered by the state and religious organizations. The state has delegated to clergy the power to solemnize legal marriages; most Protestant churches have de facto delegated to the state the power to dissolve religious marriages. Catholics and Orthodox Jews persist in refusing to give religious effect to secular divorce, thus showing that separation of the two statuses is possible if we have the will. But most Americans never distinguish religious marriage from legal marriage; the two institutions are entirely combined in our patterns of thought.

This combination of religious and secular institutions has been a problem in the debate over divorce law. It is even more problematic in the debate over same-sex marriage. Americans who think of marriage as principally a religious institution oppose same-sex marriage by large margins. Americans who think of marriage as principally a legal institution support same-sex marriage by modest majorities. Much of the first group finds it unthinkable for government to fundamentally change a religious institution; much of the second group finds it unthinkable for government to discriminate with respect to a long list of legal rights available only to married couples.

We can never resolve the debate over same-sex marriage until we separate legal marriage from religious marriage. The state should administer legal marriage, and the rules of legal marriage should be made through the political process. Religious organizations should administer religious marriages, and each religious tradition should make its own rules. Couples would choose to be religiously married, legally married, or both, or neither.

ON SEXUALITY

The battle of the sexes should not be men vs. women but modern society vs. the entrenched positions of ancient male-dominated society. Here in the 21st century, there still exist honor killings in large areas of the world, couples abort female fetuses in favor of male offspring, in Africa and the middle-east female circumcision is still practiced so that women will not enjoy the act of sex.

Men and women are equal, yet each sex has strengths and weaknesses when compared to the other, in physical prowess, mental ability, emotional capacity. Some of these are how our bodies are constructed, some from ancient historical roles. We should not be fighting against each other for dominance in the sex wars, but together to advance the whole of humanity. In much of the world women have fewer rights and freedoms compared to men, while their contributions to society are equal in breadth and depth. Women are the only means

to bring new life into the world, even with advances in
modern medical technology women are key to the
continuation of life, while men are becoming less needed.
The realm of cloning provides a means to continue life
without the application of male genetics in the fertilization
of eggs. Gender roles are blending and blurring, and
society must come to terms that gender is not digital
being either male or female, but rather analog, whith
individuals displaying a range on a scale.

ALL CHAPTER QUOTES TAKEN FROM -